STORIES FROM THE LIFE OF JESUS

Illustrated by Tony Morris

Brimax · Newmarket · England

Jesus grew up in Nazareth, where he lived with his parents. When he was twelve years old he went with them to Jerusalem for the feast of the Passover. There he spent time in the temple with the teachers, talking and listening. The teachers were surprised at how much Jesus already knew.

Jesus had a cousin called John. When John grew up, he left home to live in the wilderness near the river Jordan. There he preached the word of God and soon people flocked to listen to him and to be baptized in the river.

One day Jesus went to the river Jordan to be baptized by John.
"Will you baptize me?" asked Jesus.
"It should be you who baptizes me," replied John, who knew that Jesus was the Son of God.

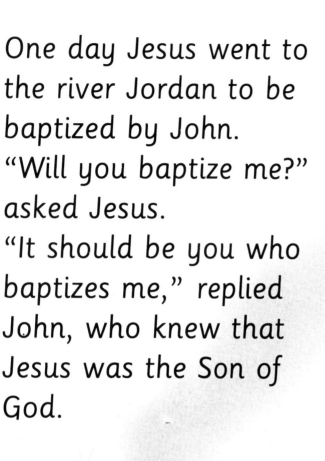

John baptized Jesus in the river Jordan and as he finished, a strange thing happened. The heavens opened and the spirit of God came down in the form of a dove. Then the people watching heard the voice of God say, "This is my Son, and I am pleased with him."

After being baptized, Jesus knew that he had God's work to do. He went to live in Galilee, where he began to tell the people about God. One day, as he walked beside the lake, Jesus met two fishermen; Simon called Peter, and Andrew. He would need help in his work so he said to the two men, "Why don't you come with me? Together we can tell the people about God."

So Peter and Andrew joined Jesus. Jesus met two more fishermen called John and James. They also joined him. Soon Jesus had chosen twelve men to help him with God's work. These men were called his disciples or the twelve apostles. They were Peter (Simon), Andrew, John, James, Philip, Thomas, Bartholomew, Matthew, James, Thaddeus, Simon and Judas Iscariot.

Jesus travelled throughout Galilee talking to the people and teaching all the time. Wherever he went, great crowds followed him. His fame spread throughout the country.

One day Jesus was on a mountain speaking to a huge crowd of people. Jesus taught them many things explaining how they should live according to the rules of God. Jesus told the people to love one another, both friend and enemy.

Jesus also taught the people how to pray, telling them to pray in simple words. Jesus said, "Pray then in this way,

> Our Father who art in Heaven,
> Hallowed be Thy name.
> Thy Kingdom come,
> Thy will be done,
> On earth as it is in Heaven.
> Give us this day our daily bread,
> And forgive us our debts,
> As we forgive our debtors.
> And lead us not into temptation
> But deliver us from evil."

This first prayer that Jesus taught has become known as the Lord's Prayer.

Jesus did many things that an ordinary person could not do. We call these 'miracles'. One of the first miracles happened at a wedding feast in the village of Cana. Jesus' mother, Mary, was also there and while all the guests were enjoying the feast, the wine ran out.

"All the wine has gone," Mary told Jesus. "Can you help? The feast will be spoiled and the bridegroom and his family are very worried."

Jesus noticed a row of empty water jars. "Fill these jars with water," he told the servants, "then pour some out for each of the guests."

The servants did as they were told. As they poured they noticed wine filling all of the cups, and not water. "Most people serve the best wine first," said one guest to the bridegroom. "You have saved the best until last."

One day a large crowd gathered to listen to Jesus preaching inside a house. Four men arrived, carrying their friend who was unable to move or walk. They tried to reach Jesus but could not find a way through the crowd. Suddenly, one of the four knew how they could reach Jesus. He climbed some steps leading to the roof and made a hole in the roof big enough for his sick friend to pass through.

Then all four friends carried the man onto the roof and with some ropes, lowered him through the hole to the feet of Jesus.

Jesus was pleased with the four friends. They had shown how they believed in him. Then everyone watched in amazement as Jesus healed the man. "Stand up from your mat and walk," said Jesus.
The man stood up and with great joy, walked away.

After this miracle, people flocked to see Jesus, bringing their family and their sick friends with them. Jesus healed many people, even lepers, who were feared by everyone. One day a leper came to Jesus. People would have nothing to do with lepers as they were afraid of catching the disease, leprosy. Jesus knew that lepers were not even allowed into the temple to pray, and he knew that this man was suffering. The man said, "I know that you can heal me," and Jesus saw that the man had faith in him, and he healed him.

Another day, a Roman soldier approached Jesus. He told him he had a servant at home who was very sick. "He is a good and kind man. I do not want him to die," said the soldier.

Jesus asked to be taken to the sick man, but the soldier said that he believed Jesus only had to say the word and the man would not die. Jesus was surprised that the soldier had such great faith, and told him to go home and he would find that the servant was well again.

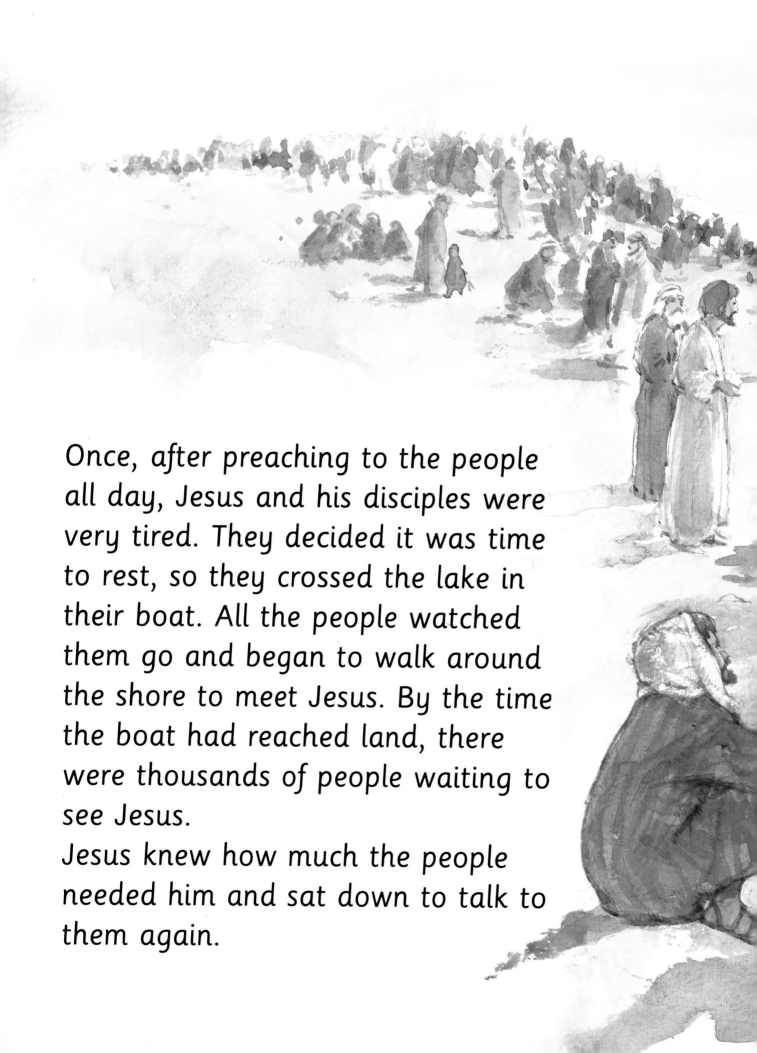

Once, after preaching to the people all day, Jesus and his disciples were very tired. They decided it was time to rest, so they crossed the lake in their boat. All the people watched them go and began to walk around the shore to meet Jesus. By the time the boat had reached land, there were thousands of people waiting to see Jesus.

Jesus knew how much the people needed him and sat down to talk to them again.

In the evening the disciples said to Jesus, "It is time to rest. The people should leave, but there is nowhere for them to stay and nothing for them to eat."

"Then we must feed them," said Jesus.

"We cannot do that," said one disciple. "There must be five thousand people here."

"Ask if anyone has any food," said Jesus. "Then bring him to me."

After a short time, a little boy was brought to Jesus. "I have five loaves and two fishes," he said. "You may have them." Jesus smiled and said, "Thank you."
The disciples then split the crowd up into groups of fifty. After this, Jesus held up the food for all to see and praised God for it.

Then Jesus handed out some bread and fish to each disciple. No one understood how but as each person was given food, there was always more for the next. Everyone was given food to eat, and all from five small loaves and two fishes.

After Jesus had fed the five thousand,
he persuaded them all to go home.
Then he went into the hills to pray.
The disciples were already rowing
back to the other side of the lake.
Jesus watched the boat
from the top of the hill
and saw that it was
struggling against the
wind. He went down the
hill to help his followers.

Jesus began to walk across the water to the boat. When the disciples saw him, they thought he was a ghost. "It is I!" cried Jesus. "Do not be afraid."

"If it is really you," said Peter, "let me walk out to you."

So Peter began to walk across the water, too. But the wind was very strong, and Peter began to sink. "Lord, save me!" he cried.

Jesus reached out his hand and saved Peter. "Why did you doubt me? Have you no faith?" he asked.

When they climbed into the boat, the wind stopped.

Many people began to believe that Jesus was the Messiah, the Son of God. Jesus talked and listened to the people. He answered their questions by telling them stories to help them understand. Mothers brought their children to Jesus so that he could bless them.

The disciples thought that Jesus had more important people to talk to than the children, but Jesus told them that no one was more important than the children. He told his disciples to let the little children come to him, and he talked to them, held them and blessed them.
To Jesus, the little ones were special.

Soon it was time for the Passover feast, the special festival celebrated by all Jews. Jesus wanted to go to Jerusalem for this special feast. He said to two disciples, "Bring me a donkey that I can ride upon."
So Jesus rode into the great city of Jerusalem on the back of a little donkey.

The people cheered and cried out,
"Hosanna! The Son of God is here!"
They threw branches and leaves at
Jesus' feet, which they had taken
from palm trees. Everyone was happy
that Jesus had arrived.

All of these appear in the pages of the story.
Can you find them?

Jesus

disciples

palm leaves

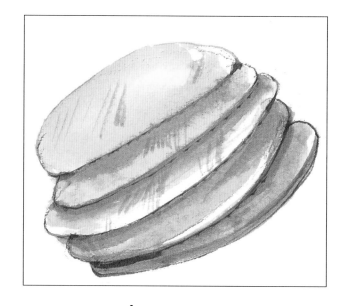

loaves